Contents

Introduction

Welcome to Mastering AI Interfacing: A Comprehensive Guide. This book is designed to be your ultimate resource for understanding and effectively working with artificial intelligence (AI). Whether you're just beginning your journey into the world of AI or you're an experienced professional looking to deepen your expertise, this guide will provide you with the tools and insights needed to navigate the rapidly evolving AI landscape.

The primary goal of this book is to demystify AI and make it accessible to everyone. We have crafted clear, practical instructions to help you interface with AI technologies, covering everything from foundational concepts to advanced techniques. By the time you reach the final chapter, you will have a solid understanding of AI and the confidence to apply AI solutions to real-world problems.

This book is designed for a diverse audience. Students and educators will find valuable resources to enhance their learning or teaching experience. Professionals and developers seeking to expand their skill set will discover practical strategies for integrating AI into their projects. Entrepreneurs and business leaders aiming to drive innovation and efficiency will gain insights into leveraging AI for transformative results. Finally, AI enthusiasts with a curiosity about this cutting-edge field will uncover a wealth of information to fuel their passion.

Artificial Intelligence refers to the simulation of human intelligence in machines that are programmed to think and learn like humans. While the concept has been around for decades, recent advancements in computing power, data availability, and algorithmic improvements have propelled AI into the forefront of technological innovation. Today, AI is reshaping industries, enhancing our daily lives, and opening up new possibilities for the future.

To appreciate the current state of AI, it's helpful to explore its evolution. The 1950s and 1960s saw the birth of AI as a field of study, focusing on symbolic reasoning and problem-solving. In the 1970s and 1980s, expert systems emerged, using rule-based approaches to mimic human decision-making. The 1990s and 2000s marked a shift toward machine learning, where systems began learning from data rather than relying solely on predefined rules. Since the 2010s, the advent of deep learning and neural networks has led to groundbreaking advancements in areas like image and speech recognition, natural language processing, and autonomous systems.

Today, AI is deeply integrated into industries such as healthcare, finance, transportation, and entertainment. These technologies enable us to analyze vast amounts of data, automate complex tasks, and generate insights that were previously unattainable. From virtual assistants like Siri and Alexa to self-driving cars and advanced medical diagnostics, AI is transforming the way we live and work.

Beyond its functional impact, AI represents a paradigm shift in how we think about problem-solving and innovation. Unlike traditional tools and systems, AI adapts, learns, and evolves over time. This dynamic nature makes it uniquely suited to address challenges that were once considered insurmountable. For instance, AI-driven technologies are being used to accelerate drug discovery, optimize supply chains, and even combat climate change through predictive modeling and resource management. As these capabilities expand, so too do the ethical and societal questions surrounding AI, from data privacy to the implications of automation on the workforce.

As you delve into the chapters ahead, you will encounter a blend of theory and practice. We will start by laying a solid foundation, introducing you to the core concepts and terminology of AI. From there, we will explore practical applications, demonstrating how to interface with popular AI platforms and tools. Real-world examples will highlight how businesses and individuals are using AI to solve complex problems and drive innovation. Hands-on exercises will give you the opportunity to apply what you've learned, ensuring that the concepts are not just understood but internalized.

Throughout this book, we will also address the broader context of AI. This includes discussing its ethical implications, potential risks, and the ways in which society can adapt to and benefit from this transformative technology. By understanding both the opportunities and challenges of AI, you will be better equipped to use it responsibly and effectively.

Whether your goal is to enhance your career, build cutting-edge applications, or simply satisfy your curiosity, this guide is here to support you. By the end of this journey, you will have gained not only the technical knowledge to interface with AI but also the strategic insights to leverage its potential in meaningful ways.

Let's dive in and unlock the immense potential of AI to create a smarter, more efficient, and equitable world. Together, we will explore the frontiers of technology and discover how AI can be a force for innovation, empowerment, and positive change.

Chapter 1: Understanding AI Basics

Artificial Intelligence (AI) often evokes images of futuristic robots or highly advanced computer systems. At its core, however, AI refers to the development of computer systems capable of performing tasks that typically require human intelligence. These tasks include learning from experience, recognizing patterns, making decisions, and understanding natural language. To fully grasp the potential of AI, it's essential to explore its definitions, types, key concepts, and applications across industries.

Artificial Intelligence can be broadly defined as the simulation of human intelligence by machines. This simulation involves programming machines to mimic cognitive functions such as problem-solving, reasoning, learning, and understanding language. AI systems are designed to either perform specific tasks (narrow AI) or emulate general human intelligence (general AI). Unlike traditional software, which relies on explicit programming for every task, AI's ability to learn and adapt from data sets it apart.

AI can be categorized based on its capability and functionality. By capability, AI is divided into narrow AI, general AI, and superintelligent AI. Narrow AI, also known as weak AI, is designed to perform specific tasks, such as virtual assistants like Siri, recommendation algorithms on Netflix, and spam filters in email systems. General AI aims to replicate human cognitive abilities across various tasks, though it remains largely theoretical. Superintelligent AI is a hypothetical stage where AI surpasses human intelligence, capable of performing tasks beyond human comprehension.

While this concept is speculative, it underscores the ambitious possibilities of AI.

When categorized by functionality, AI includes reactive machines, limited memory systems, theory-of-mind AI, and self-aware AI. Reactive machines respond to specific stimuli but lack memory and the ability to learn from past experiences, such as IBM's Deep Blue chess-playing computer. Limited memory systems use past experiences to inform future decisions and represent the majority of modern AI applications, such as self-driving cars. Theory-of-mind AI, which understands human emotions and intentions, and self-aware AI, possessing consciousness, remain theoretical concepts but serve as aspirations for future advancements.

A foundational concept in AI is machine learning (ML), which focuses on systems that learn from data and improve over time. Machine learning can be divided into supervised learning, where models learn from labeled data, and unsupervised learning, where systems identify patterns in unlabeled data. A third type, reinforcement learning, involves systems learning by trial and error to maximize performance in tasks. Each of these methods plays a vital role in enabling AI to adapt to different challenges and datasets.

Neural networks are another cornerstone of AI. Inspired by the structure of the human brain, neural networks consist of layers of interconnected nodes or "neurons" that process data. These networks are particularly effective for tasks such as image and speech recognition, where large and complex datasets are involved. Deep learning, a subset of machine learning, leverages multi-layered neural networks to address highly complex problems, from autonomous driving to natural language processing.

Natural language processing (NLP) is a critical area of AI that focuses on enabling machines to understand and respond to human language. Applications of NLP include chatbots, language translation, sentiment analysis, and virtual assistants like Alexa and Google Assistant. NLP combines computational linguistics and machine learning to analyze text and speech, bridging the gap between human communication and machine understanding.

Computer vision is another rapidly advancing field of AI, which enables machines to interpret and analyze visual data. From facial recognition systems to medical imaging and autonomous vehicles, computer vision technologies are transforming industries by making machines "see" and understand the visual world around them. AI's reliance on data and sophisticated algorithms is fundamental, requiring high-quality datasets for training and robust models to interpret that data effectively.

AI has found applications in numerous industries, revolutionizing traditional processes and creating new opportunities. In healthcare, AI assists in diagnostics, personalized medicine, and robotic surgeries. AI systems can analyze medical images to detect diseases like cancer, predict patient outcomes, and support doctors in making accurate diagnoses. The integration of AI into healthcare is not only improving efficiency but also saving lives.

In the finance sector, AI is used for fraud detection, algorithmic trading, and customer service. Machine learning models analyze financial transactions to identify anomalies, ensuring security in online banking. Predictive analytics helps institutions forecast market trends, optimize investment strategies, and tailor financial products to individual needs.

These applications are reshaping how financial services are delivered.

Transportation is another field where AI is making a profound impact. Self-driving cars rely on AI to process data from sensors and make real-time decisions, enhancing safety and efficiency on the roads. AI-powered logistics systems optimize delivery routes and manage fleet operations, reducing costs and improving reliability. Traffic management systems use AI to monitor congestion and implement dynamic solutions, improving urban mobility.

Retail industries leverage AI for personalized recommendations, inventory management, and customer service. Recommendation engines analyze customer behavior to suggest products, while AI-powered chatbots handle inquiries, streamlining the shopping experience. In manufacturing, AI enhances automation, predictive maintenance, and quality control. Robots equipped with AI can perform repetitive tasks with high precision, while predictive systems identify equipment issues before they result in downtime.

The entertainment industry benefits significantly from AI. Platforms like Netflix and Spotify use AI algorithms to deliver personalized content recommendations based on user preferences. AI is also employed in creating realistic animations, generating original music and artwork, and enhancing video game experiences. These innovations are pushing the boundaries of creativity and audience engagement.

In education, AI supports personalized learning, virtual tutoring, and automated grading. Adaptive learning systems tailor educational content to individual students' needs, enabling educators to address diverse learning styles effectively. Virtual tutors provide real-time support, and automated systems reduce administrative burdens, allowing teachers to focus more on instruction.

The energy sector is leveraging AI to optimize consumption and support renewable energy initiatives. Smart grids use AI to balance supply and demand dynamically, while predictive analytics improve the efficiency of wind and solar power generation. These technologies are crucial for advancing sustainable energy solutions and reducing environmental impact.

AI's potential extends beyond these industries into creative fields, where it acts as a collaborator rather than a replacement. Artists use AI to generate unique paintings, compose music, and even write poetry. These creative applications highlight how AI can enhance human imagination rather than stifle it. Similarly, researchers and scientists utilize AI to analyze complex data sets, accelerate discoveries, and solve problems that were previously deemed insurmountable.

One of AI's most transformative roles lies in its ability to process and analyze vast quantities of data at unprecedented speeds. In the realm of big data, AI's pattern recognition capabilities enable organizations to extract meaningful insights and trends that inform decision-making. Businesses leverage these insights to optimize operations, predict customer behavior, and stay ahead of competitors.

Another key application of AI is in cybersecurity. AI systems detect and respond to cyber threats in real-time, enhancing the security of sensitive information and critical infrastructure. Through anomaly detection and predictive analysis, AI safeguards digital environments against ever-evolving threats, ensuring that organizations remain resilient in an increasingly connected world.

Public safety and disaster management are also benefiting from AI technologies. Predictive models analyze weather patterns to anticipate natural disasters, while AI-driven drones and robots assist in search-and-rescue operations. These innovations enhance the efficiency and effectiveness of emergency responses, potentially saving lives and resources during crises.

Ethics and transparency are fundamental considerations as AI continues to permeate society. Developing AI systems that are unbiased, explainable, and aligned with human values is a priority for researchers and developers. Ethical frameworks and regulations ensure that AI technologies are deployed responsibly and equitably, fostering trust and accountability in their applications.

Understanding AI basics is a critical step toward harnessing its potential. By exploring its definitions, types, key concepts, and applications, you gain a comprehensive foundation for navigating the AI landscape. The chapters ahead will build on this knowledge, offering practical guidance and hands-on exercises to help you interface with AI technologies effectively. This foundational understanding prepares you to engage with AI not only as a tool but also as a transformative force in the modern world.

As AI continues to evolve, its impact will grow across all aspects of society. From automating routine tasks to solving complex global challenges, the potential applications are vast and diverse. By delving deeper into the concepts introduced here, you will be better equipped to contribute to and benefit from the advancements in AI. Let this chapter serve as your gateway into a fascinating and ever-expanding field.

Chapter 2: Getting Started with AI Tools

Embarking on your AI journey begins with understanding and utilizing the tools and platforms that bring artificial intelligence to life. The world of AI tools is vast and ever-expanding, catering to beginners, professionals, and enthusiasts alike. By familiarizing yourself with these tools, you can unlock AI's potential to address a myriad of challenges and opportunities.

Artificial intelligence tools vary in complexity and specialization. Whether you aim to analyze data, build machine learning models, or explore natural language processing, there's a tool tailored to your needs. This chapter will guide you through popular AI tools, provide instructions for setting them up on different operating systems, and introduce basic operations that will help you build confidence in working with AI technologies.

The AI ecosystem boasts a wide range of tools designed to cater to various levels of expertise and requirements. Among the most widely-used AI tools and platforms is TensorFlow, developed by Google, which is an open-source platform for machine learning. It provides a flexible framework for tasks such as neural network training, natural language processing, and computer vision.

PyTorch, created by Facebook, is particularly popular among researchers and developers. Its dynamic computation graphs and ease of use make it a powerful tool for deep learning projects. Similarly, Keras, built on top of TensorFlow, offers a user-friendly interface for designing neural networks, making it ideal for beginners and those seeking a simplified approach to AI development.

Another essential library is Scikit-learn, which is versatile for classical machine learning algorithms. Its features include support for regression, classification, clustering, and preprocessing. Meanwhile, OpenAI's API provides access to advanced models like GPT and DALL·E, allowing users to integrate state-of-the-art AI capabilities into applications.

For businesses, IBM Watson offers a suite of AI services tailored to enterprise needs, including natural language understanding, speech-to-text conversion, and predictive analytics. Hugging Face, known for its Transformers library, specializes in natural language processing with pre-trained models and tools for tasks like text summarization and sentiment analysis.

Google Colab is another invaluable resource. It is a free, cloud-based platform that allows you to run Python notebooks without worrying about computational limitations. It's particularly suitable for learners and professionals alike. Alongside it, Jupyter Notebook serves as an interactive development environment widely used for data analysis and visualization.

For non-programmers and business users, RapidMiner provides an accessible platform for data mining and predictive analytics, making it easier to harness AI's potential without extensive coding knowledge. RapidMiner's drag-and-drop interface simplifies complex workflows, enabling users to focus on insights rather than technical implementation.

Before diving into AI projects, you need to set up the necessary tools on your system. The installation process varies depending on the platform and operating system. For instance, to install TensorFlow on Windows or macOS, you must first install Python, verify pip, and then execute the command `pip install tensorflow`. On Linux, you can use your distribution's package manager to install Python and pip, followed by the same pip command.

Setting up PyTorch requires a slightly different approach. Its installation varies based on your system and whether you want GPU acceleration. The PyTorch website provides a tool to generate the appropriate installation command, which you can copy and execute in your terminal. GPU acceleration can significantly enhance performance, particularly for large-scale deep learning models, making this an important consideration.

Using Google Colab, however, eliminates the need for installation. By simply navigating to the Google Colab website and signing in with your Google account, you can create a new notebook and start coding immediately. This simplicity makes it an attractive option for those new to AI. Additionally, Colab provides access to free GPUs, making it a cost-effective solution for resource-intensive tasks.

Once your tools are installed, the next step is to familiarize yourself with basic operations. For example, using Scikit-learn, you can train a machine learning model by loading a dataset, splitting it into training and testing sets, training a RandomForestClassifier, and evaluating its accuracy. This step-by-step process highlights the simplicity and power of Scikit-learn for foundational AI tasks.

Hugging Face's Transformers library allows you to perform sentiment analysis by loading a pre-trained model and analyzing text with a single line of code. This ease of use makes advanced NLP tasks accessible even to those with minimal coding experience. For instance, you can quickly classify text, summarize articles, or translate languages without extensive model training.

OpenAI's API enables you to generate text by connecting to their service with an API key and crafting prompts for tasks like explaining concepts or summarizing content. This powerful tool provides flexibility and creativity, enabling developers to build applications that range from chatbots to content creation platforms.

To further expand your capabilities, you can explore advanced features of these tools. TensorFlow, for example, supports custom training loops, which provide fine-grained control over model training. PyTorch's ecosystem includes libraries like TorchVision for computer vision and TorchText for NLP, allowing seamless integration of specialized functionalities.

Troubleshooting common issues is another critical skill in your AI journey. Dependency conflicts, for example, can be managed by using virtual environments. You can create one with `python -m venv env` and activate it before installing packages. This isolates your project dependencies, preventing conflicts with other tools or libraries.

For resource-intensive tasks, cloud platforms like Google Colab or AWS provide scalable solutions. Colab's ability to connect with Google Drive ensures seamless access to your data and models, while AWS offers a range of services like SageMaker for deploying and managing AI models in production environments.

Permission errors during installation can often be resolved by running commands with administrative privileges or adding `--user` to pip commands. These small adjustments ensure smooth setup and operation of your AI tools. Additionally, keeping your tools and libraries updated minimizes compatibility issues and provides access to the latest features.

Learning to use AI tools is a vital step in becoming proficient in artificial intelligence. By understanding the capabilities of each tool, setting up your development environment, and practicing basic operations, you lay the foundation for more complex AI projects. The tools and techniques covered in this chapter are your gateway to unlocking the transformative potential of AI.

The journey may seem challenging at first, but with consistent practice and exploration, the possibilities are boundless. Whether you're training machine learning models, analyzing data, or developing creative AI applications, these tools empower you to innovate and excel in the dynamic field of AI. By mastering these foundational skills, you position yourself to tackle real-world problems and contribute to the evolving landscape of artificial intelligence.

In addition to technical expertise, cultivating a problem-solving mindset is essential. AI projects often involve iterative experimentation and refinement. Embracing this process will enhance your ability to adapt and succeed in diverse scenarios. Each challenge you overcome strengthens your proficiency and deepens your understanding of AI concepts.

The potential applications of AI tools extend far beyond traditional domains. From healthcare to entertainment, AI is revolutionizing industries and creating new opportunities. Understanding the societal impact of AI is crucial as you progress, ensuring ethical considerations are integrated into your work.

In the chapters ahead, we will delve deeper into advanced techniques and real-world applications, further solidifying your expertise. By building on the knowledge gained here, you will be equipped to navigate the complexities of AI development with confidence and creativity. The tools you've explored are just the beginning—a gateway to a future defined by innovation and possibility.

Chapter 3: Data Preparation for AI

Data is the backbone of any AI system. The quality and quantity of data directly influence the performance and accuracy of AI models. Without good data, even the most sophisticated algorithms can fail to deliver meaningful results. Training AI models requires large volumes of relevant data. The more robust the dataset, the better the model can generalize to new and unseen scenarios. Moreover, high-quality data minimizes errors and improves the precision of AI predictions. Through the identification of patterns, data empowers AI systems to make informed decisions, while proper preparation ensures fairness and reduces bias, which is critical for maintaining trust in AI systems.

Collecting data is the first step in the data preparation process. Various methods can be employed based on the type of AI application and domain. Surveys and questionnaires offer direct insights by gathering data from individuals, while web scraping allows for automated extraction of data from online sources. APIs serve as a gateway to structured datasets from various online services, enabling seamless integration with AI workflows. IoT devices and sensors are increasingly popular for capturing real-time data in fields like healthcare and smart cities. Public datasets from government archives or research institutions provide readily available resources. For specific or niche requirements, manual data entry remains a reliable but time-intensive method.

Once data is collected, it must be cleaned and preprocessed to ensure it is suitable for AI training. Data cleaning involves handling missing values, which can be addressed through deletion, imputation, or the use of tolerant algorithms. Removing duplicates is essential to maintain data integrity and avoid redundancy. Correcting errors, whether they are typographical mistakes or outliers, ensures the dataset's reliability. These steps establish a solid foundation for further processing.

Data transformation techniques further refine the dataset. Normalization scales numerical data to a standard range, ensuring consistent input for machine learning models. Standardization, on the other hand, adjusts data to have a mean of zero and a standard deviation of one, which is particularly useful for algorithms assuming normally distributed inputs. Encoding categorical data—converting textual or ordinal categories into numerical representations—is another critical step. Techniques such as one-hot encoding or label encoding simplify the incorporation of categorical features into AI models.

Feature engineering amplifies the value of raw data. Creating new features from existing data often uncovers hidden patterns that enhance model performance. For instance, extracting the "day of the week" from a timestamp can reveal time-based trends. Feature selection narrows down the dataset to include only the most relevant variables, reducing dimensionality and computational overhead.

Data splitting divides the dataset into training, validation, and test sets. This step ensures that the model's performance is evaluated accurately. A typical split might allocate 70-80% of the data for training, 10-15% for validation, and the remainder for testing. This division allows for iterative model improvement and prevents overfitting.

Data augmentation generates synthetic data to enhance the existing dataset. This technique is especially valuable when data is scarce. Approaches such as oversampling, undersampling, and using generative models expand the dataset's diversity without compromising its integrity. Synthetic data generation bolsters model training by exposing it to a broader range of scenarios.

The iterative process of data preparation often reveals the nuances of the dataset. Exploring the data's structure through visualization tools like histograms or scatter plots uncovers distributions, correlations, and anomalies. These insights inform subsequent steps in the preparation pipeline, enabling tailored strategies for cleaning, transforming, and splitting data.

Balancing datasets is another essential aspect. Imbalanced data can skew AI models towards over-represented classes, reducing their effectiveness in real-world applications. Techniques like SMOTE (Synthetic Minority Oversampling Technique) create balanced datasets by generating synthetic samples for minority classes. This balance is critical for fair and unbiased AI systems.

Scalability is a growing concern in data preparation. As datasets expand, traditional methods may struggle to handle the volume efficiently. Tools like Apache Spark and Hadoop offer distributed processing capabilities, ensuring that large-scale datasets are managed effectively. These platforms facilitate preprocessing tasks such as filtering, aggregation, and transformation on massive datasets. This scalability allows AI developers to process data faster and more efficiently, reducing the time needed for model training.

An often-overlooked aspect is documentation. Maintaining a comprehensive record of data sources, preprocessing steps, and transformations ensures reproducibility and transparency. Detailed documentation allows teams to trace decisions, debug issues, and collaborate effectively. This practice also aligns with ethical AI development by fostering accountability.

Ethical considerations play a pivotal role in data preparation. Ensuring data privacy and compliance with regulations such as GDPR (General Data Protection Regulation) and CCPA (California Consumer Privacy Act) is non-negotiable. Anonymizing sensitive data and obtaining informed consent are fundamental to ethical data handling. Bias mitigation during data preparation further reinforces fairness and inclusivity. Beyond compliance, fostering diversity in datasets helps avoid perpetuating harmful stereotypes or biases that can emerge when data fails to represent all demographics equally.

The tools available for data preparation range from general-purpose programming languages like Python to specialized platforms. Libraries such as Pandas and NumPy simplify data manipulation tasks, while Scikit-learn offers robust preprocessing modules. For visualizing data, tools like Matplotlib and Seaborn provide clear and informative representations of complex datasets. Additionally, machine learning platforms like TensorFlow and PyTorch offer built-in utilities for handling data preprocessing as part of the larger AI pipeline.

Cloud platforms offer scalable solutions for data preparation. Services like Google Cloud DataPrep and AWS Glue provide user-friendly interfaces for cleaning and transforming data. These platforms integrate seamlessly with other cloud-based tools, streamlining the end-to-end AI workflow. Their ability to handle large datasets makes them indispensable in modern AI development. These cloud platforms also offer automated scaling, ensuring that computing resources match the demands of the dataset without manual intervention.

Automated machine learning (AutoML) frameworks increasingly incorporate automated data preparation. These frameworks identify optimal preprocessing techniques, reducing the time and expertise required for manual intervention. AutoML democratizes AI development, making advanced capabilities accessible to non-experts. However, while AutoML can simplify the process, human expertise is still needed to ensure that the data used is accurate and free of biases that could impact the model's fairness.

Data preparation challenges are inevitable, but proactive strategies can mitigate their impact. Missing or incomplete data requires thoughtful imputation strategies. Noisy data can be filtered or smoothed using statistical methods. Tools for anomaly detection, such as Isolation Forests, help identify and address outliers. Data preprocessing tools often come with pre-built functions to help manage common data issues, but custom solutions may still be necessary for complex or highly specialized data.

Collaboration during data preparation enhances quality and efficiency. Cross-functional teams contribute diverse perspectives, ensuring datasets are comprehensive and representative. Collaborative platforms like Jupyter Notebooks facilitate teamwork, providing shared environments for code, visualization, and documentation. Team collaboration not only improves the accuracy of data processing but also helps to identify any overlooked biases or gaps in the dataset that could affect model performance.

Iterative validation during data preparation ensures alignment with project goals. Regular checkpoints validate the dataset's quality and relevance, preventing downstream issues during model training. This iterative approach aligns with the agile methodology, fostering adaptability and continuous improvement. Frequent feedback from model performance on validation sets can also inform necessary adjustments to the data preparation process, refining both the data and the model over time.

Properly prepared data is foundational to AI's success. The meticulous efforts invested in cleaning, transforming, and splitting data translate into more accurate and reliable models. This preparation not only enhances technical outcomes but also builds trust in AI solutions by ensuring fairness and transparency. Moreover, prepared data allows AI models to scale effectively as new data is introduced, providing long-term viability for AI applications.

The skills acquired during data preparation extend beyond AI development. Mastery of data manipulation, visualization, and ethical considerations equips professionals with versatile capabilities applicable across domains. These skills form the bedrock of data-driven decision-making, a cornerstone of modern innovation. Moreover, as AI systems are increasingly used in a variety of industries, the demand for skilled professionals in data preparation will continue to rise, making this expertise invaluable.

In conclusion, data preparation is not merely a precursor to AI training; it is an integral component that defines the project's success. By embracing best practices, leveraging tools, and prioritizing ethics, data preparation empowers AI practitioners to unlock the full potential of artificial intelligence. The evolving nature of data and technology will continue to challenge data preparation techniques, but those who master this process will be at the forefront of AI innovation.

Chapter 4: Building Your First AI Model

The journey of building your first AI model begins with a fundamental question: what problem are you trying to solve? This question may seem simple, but the answer determines every decision that follows. Identifying a problem suitable for AI requires thoughtful consideration of its scope and impact.

Relevance is the first criterion. The problem you choose should align with your field of work, study, or personal interest. AI projects can be complex and time-consuming, and aligning the project with your passions or career goals will keep you motivated when challenges arise.

Feasibility is another critical consideration. Even the most exciting problem is useless if you lack the resources to tackle it. Do you have access to the necessary data? Are your computational resources sufficient to train an AI model? Do you have the time to dedicate to this project? Assessing these factors early on can save you time and frustration later.

Impact is also worth evaluating. Solving a problem with significant consequences can be immensely rewarding. Whether you're addressing a business need, improving efficiency, or solving a social issue, aim to work on something meaningful. AI has the power to transform lives—choose a problem where this potential can be realized.

Finally, clarity and specificity in defining the problem are essential. AI works best when given a clear and well-defined objective. For instance, instead of tackling "improving healthcare," narrow it down to something actionable, like predicting patient readmission rates or identifying anomalies in medical imaging.

Once your problem is defined, the next step is to understand the types of AI models available and how they relate to your chosen problem. Broadly, AI models fall into several categories, each with its strengths and use cases.

Supervised learning models are among the most common. These models learn from labeled data—data where the input is paired with the correct output. Examples include regression models for predicting numerical values and classification models for categorizing inputs into predefined groups.

Unsupervised learning, by contrast, works with unlabeled data. These models identify hidden patterns or groupings in data. Clustering algorithms, such as k-means, are often used to segment customers or analyze behavioral patterns. Dimensionality reduction techniques, like Principal Component Analysis (PCA), simplify complex datasets for visualization or analysis.

Reinforcement learning operates on a different principle. It learns through interaction, receiving feedback in the form of rewards or penalties. This approach is especially effective in dynamic environments, such as training game-playing agents or teaching robots to perform tasks.

Deep learning, a subset of machine learning, is renowned for its ability to handle complex problems. Using neural networks with multiple layers, it excels at processing unstructured data like images, audio, and text. Convolutional Neural Networks (CNNs) are widely used for image-related tasks, while Recurrent Neural Networks (RNNs) are popular in sequence analysis, such as natural language processing.

Now that you understand the types of models, it's time to move into the practical steps of creating your first AI model. This process begins with problem definition. Clearly state what you aim to solve, identify the input data, and specify the desired output. For example, if your goal is to predict house prices, your inputs might include features like location, size, and number of rooms, while the output is the predicted price.

Data collection follows. Data is the foundation of any AI model, and its quality directly impacts the outcome. Your dataset should be comprehensive and relevant to the problem at hand. Gathering this data often involves accessing public datasets, using APIs, or leveraging internal business data.

Raw data, however, is rarely ready for modeling. Data cleaning and preprocessing are essential to remove inconsistencies, handle missing values, and ensure the data is in a usable format. Techniques like normalization, standardization, and feature engineering can further enhance data quality and relevance.

With data prepared, the next step is selecting an appropriate model. This decision depends on the nature of the problem and the available data. For instance, if you're predicting continuous values, a linear regression model may be appropriate. If you're classifying images, a deep learning model like a CNN might be the best choice.

Data splitting is a crucial step in the modeling process. Dividing your dataset into training, validation, and test sets ensures that your model is evaluated fairly and avoids overfitting. The training set teaches the model, the validation set tunes it, and the test set evaluates its generalization performance.

Model training is where the magic happens. Using the training data, the model adjusts its parameters to minimize error. This process often involves iterative optimization techniques, like gradient descent, to refine the model's accuracy. Libraries like TensorFlow, PyTorch, and scikit-learn simplify this process, allowing you to focus on the results.

Validation is the next step. By using the validation set, you can fine-tune your model's hyperparameters—settings that control the learning process. Techniques like cross-validation and grid search can help find the optimal configuration, preventing overfitting and improving performance.

Once the model performs well on the validation set, it's time for testing. Testing evaluates the model's ability to generalize to completely unseen data. Metrics such as accuracy, precision, recall, and mean squared error provide a detailed understanding of its performance.

If the test results are satisfactory, the final step is deployment. Deployment involves integrating the trained model into a real-world application, where it can make predictions on new data. This step often requires additional considerations, such as scalability, latency, and user interface design.

Evaluating model performance doesn't stop after deployment. Continuous monitoring is essential to ensure the model remains effective as new data or challenges emerge. Retraining the model periodically can help adapt to these changes, maintaining its accuracy and relevance.

Understanding evaluation metrics is key to this process. Accuracy measures the proportion of correct predictions, but for imbalanced datasets, precision and recall provide a more nuanced view. These metrics, combined into the F1 score, offer a balanced performance indicator.

For regression problems, Mean Squared Error (MSE) quantifies prediction accuracy by measuring the average squared difference between predicted and actual values. In classification tasks, confusion matrices reveal detailed insights into true positives, false positives, true negatives, and false negatives.

Advanced evaluation tools like the Receiver Operating Characteristic (ROC) curve and its associated Area Under the Curve (AUC) score further aid in assessing model performance, particularly in binary classification problems.

Iterative improvement is the cornerstone of AI development. Each stage—data collection, model selection, training, validation, and testing—offers opportunities for refinement. Embrace this iterative mindset, learning from mistakes and building on successes.

As you build your first AI model, remember that perfection is not the goal. Instead, focus on gaining hands-on experience and understanding the principles of AI. Each project, no matter how small, adds to your expertise and prepares you for more ambitious challenges.

AI is as much an art as it is a science. Creativity and problem-solving are at its heart. With persistence, curiosity, and a willingness to learn, you'll find yourself not only building AI models but also discovering innovative ways to use them to change the world.

Chapter 5: Advanced AI Techniques

Artificial Intelligence (AI) has rapidly progressed from a nascent field to one of the most transformative technologies of the modern age. Foundational concepts like supervised and unsupervised learning provide the bedrock for AI systems. However, advanced techniques offer the means to truly push boundaries, enabling AI systems to tackle complex, real-world challenges that were previously insurmountable. This chapter explores some of the most impactful advanced AI methods, serving as a comprehensive guide for those aspiring to become experts in the field.

Transfer learning stands out as one of the most effective tools in an AI practitioner's arsenal. At its core, transfer learning involves leveraging a pre-trained model—one that has already learned a wealth of knowledge from one task—to improve performance on another, often related, task. For instance, a model pre-trained on billions of internet images can be fine-tuned to classify medical images with minimal additional training data. This ability to reuse learned features offers several advantages. It significantly reduces training time since the model doesn't need to learn everything from scratch. Moreover, it improves accuracy, especially when the target dataset is small or lacks diversity.

A key tip for applying transfer learning is to analyze the similarity between the source and target tasks. The closer they are in nature, the better the results. For example, using a language model pre-trained on English text might not yield optimal results if the target task involves processing Chinese text unless additional fine-tuning is performed. Practitioners should also pay attention to the layers being fine-tuned; freezing earlier layers (which capture general features) while adjusting later layers (which are task-specific) often yields the best outcomes.

One of the subtler challenges in transfer learning is understanding the limits of pre-trained models. While these models excel in many tasks, their biases—often inherited from the large datasets they were trained on—can sometimes hinder performance. For instance, an image recognition model pre-trained on Western-centric datasets might perform poorly when tasked with identifying culturally specific objects or phenomena. To counteract this, practitioners should consider augmenting the target dataset with diverse samples or employing domain adaptation techniques.

In contrast to transfer learning, which relies on pre-trained knowledge, reinforcement learning (RL) focuses on learning from interaction with an environment. Here, an agent learns to make a sequence of decisions by maximizing cumulative rewards over time. RL has achieved legendary status in AI, largely due to its groundbreaking applications in games like Chess, Go, and StarCraft. The successes of AlphaGo and OpenAI Five exemplify the power of RL in environments where strategy, adaptation, and long-term planning are key.

Understanding RL involves grasping a few core concepts. The agent is the decision-making entity, the environment is the space in which the agent operates, and the reward signal is the feedback the agent receives for its actions. A simple analogy is training a dog to fetch a ball: the dog (agent) interacts with its surroundings (environment) and receives treats (rewards) for successfully fetching the ball. Tips for RL include ensuring that reward signals are well-designed—poorly constructed rewards can lead to unintended behaviors, as the agent optimizes for outcomes that might not align with the intended goal.

One of RL's most exciting areas is in real-world applications beyond gaming. For example, in financial technology, RL is used to design adaptive trading algorithms that learn to maximize returns in volatile markets. In healthcare, RL-based systems optimize treatment plans for patients by dynamically adjusting therapies based on their responses. When applying RL to real-world tasks, it is crucial to incorporate safety mechanisms. For instance, in robotics, designing fail-safes to prevent harm during exploration is essential for deploying RL agents in physical environments.

Moving into the realm of creativity, Generative Adversarial Networks (GANs) have become a cornerstone of generative AI. Comprising two neural networks—a generator and a discriminator—GANs operate on an adversarial principle. The generator creates synthetic data, while the discriminator evaluates its authenticity. This tug-of-war drives the generator to produce outputs that are increasingly indistinguishable from real data.

One of the most fascinating applications of GANs is in art and design. Artists and designers have used GANs to generate unique patterns, artwork, and even entire virtual worlds. For instance, GANs have been employed to create realistic human faces from scratch, which are indistinguishable from actual photographs. Beyond aesthetics, GANs are invaluable in data augmentation. By generating synthetic samples, they help address class imbalances in datasets, which is a common challenge in machine learning. When working with GANs, a useful trick is to carefully monitor the balance between the generator and discriminator during training; if one network outpaces the other, the adversarial process can collapse, leading to suboptimal results.

GANs are also finding applications in areas like anomaly detection, where they generate data to represent "normal" scenarios, enabling systems to identify deviations more effectively. In the medical field, GANs are used to create synthetic MRI scans or X-rays to help train diagnostic models without compromising patient privacy. A tip for using GANs in sensitive domains is to validate the generated data rigorously; ensuring ethical and accurate representation is critical, especially when the outputs impact decision-making in healthcare or security.

As AI systems grow more sophisticated, so too does the demand for transparency. Explainable AI (XAI) aims to make AI systems more interpretable, ensuring users can understand why a particular decision was made. In industries like healthcare, finance, and law, understanding why an AI model made a decision is often as important as the decision itself. Techniques such as LIME (Local Interpretable Model-agnostic Explanations) and SHAP (SHapley Additive exPlanations) provide insights into how models generate predictions. For example, SHAP assigns each feature a contribution score, highlighting its impact on the final decision.

One practical example is in healthcare. An AI system recommending treatment plans can use SHAP or LIME to highlight the most important factors—such as specific symptoms or test results—behind its recommendations. Doctors can then use this information to make informed decisions, ensuring AI augments rather than replaces their expertise. A helpful tip for developers working with XAI is to involve domain experts early in the design process. Their input ensures that explanations are meaningful and aligned with real-world decision-making processes.

Another critical aspect of advanced AI is hyperparameter tuning. The performance of AI models often hinges on the choice of hyperparameters—those configuration settings that are not learned during training but must be specified beforehand. Examples include learning rate, batch size, and the number of layers in a neural network. While manual tuning is feasible for small models, it becomes impractical for larger architectures. Techniques like grid search, random search, and Bayesian optimization automate this process. Grid search exhaustively evaluates all combinations of parameters within a defined range, while random search samples parameters randomly, often yielding comparable results with fewer iterations.

Federated learning is another innovative approach shaping the future of AI. By distributing training across devices, it ensures data privacy while leveraging computational resources at the edge. A growing application is in autonomous vehicles, where federated learning enables car manufacturers to improve navigation algorithms without centralizing sensitive location data. Combined with cryptographic methods like secure multi-party computation, federated learning can deliver robust and secure AI solutions.

In 2019, a small tech startup based in Nairobi, Kenya, faced a unique challenge: creating an AI-powered crop diagnosis system to help farmers identify diseases in plants. The team, while skilled, didn't have the resources to gather and label thousands of images of local crops affected by diseases. Instead, they turned to transfer learning. Using a pre-trained convolutional neural network (CNN) model trained on a massive dataset like ImageNet, they fine-tuned it with just a few hundred images of cassava leaves—each labeled by agricultural experts.

The results were astonishing. Within weeks, the system achieved over 90% accuracy in diagnosing common crop diseases. Farmers reported a significant reduction in crop losses, and the startup gained international recognition for its innovative use of AI. The key takeaway? Transfer learning empowered a small team with limited data to create a transformative tool. For practitioners, this story underscores the power of leveraging existing models to achieve remarkable outcomes with minimal resources.

Reinforcement learning isn't just about training machines—it mirrors the way humans and animals learn through trial and error. Picture this: A child learning to ride a bike falls multiple times but eventually masters the skill through persistence and positive reinforcement from parents. Similarly, RL agents "fall" (make suboptimal decisions) repeatedly during training, but with the right feedback (rewards), they learn to balance their metaphorical bikes.

In 2017, researchers at Google DeepMind trained a two-legged robot to walk using RL algorithms. At first, the robot stumbled hilariously, flailing its limbs in every direction. Over time, it learned to take stable, coordinated steps. This progression not only reveals the technical marvel of RL but also evokes empathy for the "learning" machine, illustrating how AI mimics human development.

Chapter 6: Interfacing with AI

In a world where artificial intelligence (AI) is seamlessly integrated into everyday life, understanding how to effectively interface with these systems has become a critical skill. Whether you are a developer building applications, a business leader deploying AI solutions, or a user leveraging AI tools, mastering the art of interaction ensures you get the most out of this transformative technology.

AI interfaces serve as the bridge between humans and machines, translating natural inputs—such as text, voice, or gestures—into actions and responses. A well-designed interface enhances usability and accessibility while minimizing frustration. Depending on the application, interfaces can range from graphical user interfaces (GUIs) to APIs and voice assistants. These interfaces are the conduits through which AI's capabilities are made accessible to users, and they play a pivotal role in shaping the overall experience.

Graphical User Interfaces (GUIs) are visual interfaces, often involving buttons, sliders, and text boxes. Examples include AI-powered photo editing apps or recommendation engines embedded in e-commerce websites. These interfaces are best suited for users who interact visually with systems and benefit from a user-friendly design. A GUI's effectiveness depends on its ability to simplify complex AI functions into straightforward actions that users can perform effortlessly. Developers need to focus on intuitive design and seamless integration to ensure that GUIs enhance rather than hinder the user experience.

Application Programming Interfaces (APIs), on the other hand, enable developers to integrate AI functionality into software or applications. APIs are often used in backend systems, allowing seamless automation and scalability, and are commonly utilized for tasks like natural language processing (NLP), computer vision, or machine learning predictions. APIs act as the hidden connectors behind many modern AI applications, enabling data flow and functionality that may not be visible to end users but is essential for the system's operation.

Voice interfaces, such as those offered by Alexa, Google Assistant, and Siri, allow users to interact with AI using spoken language. These are ideal for hands-free operations or accessibility-focused solutions. Voice interfaces require careful attention to natural language processing capabilities to ensure they can understand and respond accurately to user commands. As voice-based systems evolve, they are becoming more adept at handling nuanced and context-dependent instructions, making them invaluable tools for many applications.

Command-Line Interfaces (CLIs) are text-based and typically used by technical users for direct interaction with AI models or systems. These interfaces are especially useful for scripting, testing, or rapid prototyping. While CLIs may lack the visual appeal of GUIs, their simplicity and power make them indispensable for developers and engineers who need precise control over AI systems.

A successful AI interface begins with a clear understanding of the target audience. Developers and designers should ask questions like: Who will use this interface? What are their technical skills and preferences? What problem are they trying to solve? By answering these questions, you can tailor the interface to meet the needs of its users effectively. Understanding the user's context and expectations is the foundation of designing an interface that is both functional and engaging.

Usability is key to a successful AI system. For GUIs, prioritize clarity in layout and navigation. For voice or text-based systems, design conversational flows that feel natural. APIs should come with comprehensive documentation and examples to ensure developers can easily integrate and use them. Ensuring that the interface is intuitive minimizes frustration and enhances user satisfaction. Usability testing should be an ongoing process, incorporating feedback from diverse user groups to refine the system continuously.

AI systems are often described as black boxes, which can create mistrust among users. To build confidence, interfaces must offer transparency. This includes explaining how decisions are made, providing actionable feedback to user inputs, and offering error messages that clarify rather than confuse. Transparency and explainability help users understand and trust the AI's functionality. For instance, a recommendation engine might display the factors influencing its suggestions, helping users feel more in control of their interactions with the system.

Error handling and recovery are critical components of any AI interface. Inevitably, users will encounter situations where the AI fails to meet expectations. Planning for these scenarios involves allowing users to correct errors or try alternative inputs, clearly communicating the system's limitations or uncertainties, and logging errors for developers to analyze and improve performance. A robust error-handling strategy ensures a smoother user experience and helps refine the system over time. Effective error messages should not only identify the issue but also guide users on how to resolve it.

Various tools can simplify the process of interfacing with AI. No-code platforms like Bubble, Airtable, or Lobe enable users to deploy AI systems without writing code. These platforms often include drag-and-drop interfaces, making interaction more accessible to non-technical users. They lower the barrier to entry for businesses and individuals who want to harness the power of AI without investing heavily in technical resources. For developers, software development kits (SDKs) and frameworks like TensorFlow.js, PyTorch, or OpenAI APIs provide robust tools for integrating and customizing AI. These tools allow for a high degree of flexibility and are essential for creating bespoke solutions tailored to specific use cases.

Building custom applications tailored to specific needs offers greater flexibility and can enhance the user experience. Custom interfaces allow organizations to align AI tools closely with their workflows, ensuring maximum efficiency and user satisfaction. Whether it's a chatbot designed to handle customer service queries or a predictive analytics dashboard for business intelligence, custom solutions can provide a competitive edge by addressing unique challenges.

When designing AI interfaces, it's important to start simple. Begin with minimal features and expand based on user feedback. Overloading the interface with too many options or functionalities can overwhelm users and reduce adoption rates. Iteration and improvement are essential; use analytics and user data to refine the interface over time. Prioritize accessibility to ensure that the interface accommodates diverse user needs, including those with disabilities. Inclusive design is not just a social responsibility but also a strategic advantage, as it broadens the potential user base.

Regularly testing the interface with real users helps identify potential pain points and ensures that the system evolves to meet user expectations. Testing should include a mix of usability studies, performance evaluations, and accessibility assessments. Collecting qualitative and quantitative data during these tests provides valuable insights that can guide future development efforts.

As AI technology advances, interfaces will become increasingly adaptive and intuitive. Emerging trends in AI interfaces include context-aware systems that adapt based on user behavior or environmental factors. For example, a context-aware AI could adjust its suggestions or outputs based on the user's location, time of day, or activity. This level of personalization enhances user engagement and satisfaction by delivering more relevant and timely interactions.

Augmented reality (AR) and virtual reality (VR) offer immersive environments powered by AI to enhance learning, gaming, or productivity. AI-driven AR applications can provide real-time insights and overlays, such as identifying objects in a user's field of view or offering step-by-step instructions for complex tasks. In VR, AI can create dynamic and responsive environments that adapt to the user's actions, making experiences more engaging and realistic.

Emotionally intelligent AI is another exciting development, with interfaces that detect and respond to emotional cues for more personalized interactions. By analyzing facial expressions, tone of voice, or text sentiment, these systems can adapt their responses to better suit the user's mood or intentions. Such capabilities have significant potential in areas like mental health support, customer service, and education.

Interfacing with AI is both an art and a science. By focusing on usability, transparency, and adaptability, you can create systems that empower users and unlock the full potential of AI. Mastering the principles of effective interaction ensures that AI systems remain valuable tools that enhance human capabilities and transform industries. As the field of AI continues to evolve, so too will the methods and strategies for building effective interfaces, making this an ongoing area of exploration and innovation.

Chapter 7: Personal Privacy and AI

In today's digital age, artificial intelligence (AI) has woven itself into nearly every aspect of our lives. From shaping how we communicate to transforming how we shop, its influence is pervasive and undeniable. Yet, alongside these remarkable advancements, AI has introduced profound challenges, particularly regarding personal privacy. The convenience and capabilities it brings come at the cost of heightened vulnerability to data misuse. This chapter explores the nuanced interplay between personal privacy and AI, shedding light on the risks, dilemmas, and strategies necessary to safeguard personal information in an increasingly data-driven world.

Personal privacy has long been regarded as the right to keep one's information secure and free from unauthorized access. However, in the era of AI, this concept has evolved significantly. Privacy now encompasses not only the protection of personal data but also the ethical considerations surrounding its use. AI systems thrive on vast datasets, which often include sensitive details such as browsing habits, purchase histories, health records, and financial transactions. The reliance on such data raises essential questions about how much privacy individuals are expected to forfeit for the convenience of advanced technology.

The challenges to personal privacy in the AI landscape are multifaceted, beginning with the sheer scale of data collection. AI systems require enormous datasets to function effectively, and these are often gathered from various sources, sometimes without explicit consent. Websites, apps, and smart devices collect information constantly, creating detailed profiles that fuel AI algorithms. However, the storage of such data, if not adequately secured, presents a significant risk. Data breaches have become alarmingly common, exposing sensitive information to malicious actors and eroding public trust.

Equally troubling is the widespread sharing and usage of personal data. Many companies share collected data with third parties for purposes such as targeted advertising, research, or partnership initiatives. While this practice may be framed as a way to enhance user experiences, it often occurs with minimal transparency. Misuse of this shared data or unauthorized access can lead to severe repercussions for individuals, including identity theft or unwarranted profiling.

Profiling, in particular, is a double-edged sword in the world of AI. By analyzing patterns in data, AI can create intricate profiles of individuals, predicting behaviors, preferences, and even potential vulnerabilities. While this capability can be used for personalized recommendations or security measures, it can also cross ethical boundaries. When profiles are used for surveillance or behavioral manipulation, they infringe upon personal freedoms and privacy, undermining the trust between individuals and organizations.

Algorithmic bias further complicates these issues. AI systems are only as unbiased as the data they are trained on. If datasets reflect societal prejudices, AI will inevitably perpetuate those biases. This can result in unfair treatment of individuals based on race, gender, or socioeconomic status. For instance, biased algorithms may influence decisions in hiring, lending, or law enforcement, reinforcing existing inequalities while exacerbating privacy concerns.

To address these risks, strategies for protecting personal privacy must be robust and multifaceted.

Transparency and consent are critical starting points. Organizations must clearly communicate what data is being collected, why it is needed, and how it will be used. Explicit consent should be sought before data collection, empowering users to make informed decisions.

Data minimization is another crucial principle. Collecting only the data necessary for a specific AI function can limit exposure to unnecessary risks. Excessive or irrelevant data collection not only wastes resources but also increases the potential for misuse.

Anonymization and encryption are powerful tools in protecting personal information. Anonymization involves removing identifying details from data, making it difficult to trace back to individuals. Encryption, on the other hand, secures data during storage and transmission, ensuring that even if unauthorized parties gain access, the information remains unintelligible.

Regular audits and assessments of AI systems are also essential. These evaluations help ensure compliance with privacy regulations, identify vulnerabilities, and promote accountability. By systematically reviewing AI operations, organizations can detect and mitigate risks before they escalate into significant breaches.

Providing users with control over their data is another critical step. Features that allow individuals to access, modify, or delete their information not only enhance transparency but also foster trust. When users feel empowered to manage their data, they are more likely to engage with AI systems confidently.

Ethical considerations should underpin every stage of AI development. This includes addressing biases in datasets, designing fair algorithms, and prioritizing user privacy. Ethical AI development aligns technological innovation with societal values, ensuring that progress does not come at the expense of individual rights.

Legal and regulatory frameworks play an indispensable role in safeguarding personal privacy. For instance, the General Data Protection Regulation (GDPR) in the European Union sets stringent guidelines for data collection, storage, and usage. By emphasizing transparency and accountability, GDPR has become a global benchmark for data protection.

In the United States, the California Consumer Privacy Act (CCPA) empowers consumers with rights over their personal data. These include the right to know what data is collected and the right to opt out of data sales. Similarly, the Health Insurance Portability and Accountability Act (HIPAA) protects sensitive health information, establishing standards for secure handling and transmission.

As AI continues to evolve, the importance of personal privacy cannot be overstated. The stakes are high: without careful management, the very tools designed to enhance our lives could erode our most fundamental rights. By understanding the risks and implementing effective strategies, individuals and organizations can navigate the complexities of AI responsibly.

The key lies in balancing innovation with ethical considerations. Technology should serve humanity, not compromise it. Safeguarding personal privacy is not merely a legal obligation—it is a moral imperative that ensures AI remains a force for good in an interconnected world.

Chapter 8: Troubleshooting and Optimization

In the rapidly evolving field of artificial intelligence, ensuring smooth and efficient interactions with AI systems is crucial. As AI technology becomes increasingly integrated into various aspects of daily life and business operations, the ability to troubleshoot issues and optimize performance is essential for achieving the desired outcomes. This chapter delves into the key practices necessary for addressing common problems and fine-tuning AI systems to deliver optimal results.

When working with AI systems, users may encounter several challenges that can hinder effective interaction. Inaccurate responses are one of the most common issues, often arising from insufficient training data, ambiguous queries, or limitations within the AI model itself. For example, a model may fail to provide a relevant answer if it has not been adequately trained on the subject matter or if the user's input is vague. Another frequent problem is slow performance, which can stem from high server load, inefficient algorithms, or network latency. These delays not only frustrate users but also impact the usability of the system.

Misunderstandings are another significant hurdle, where AI systems misinterpret user input due to language nuances, slang, or complex sentence structures. This issue highlights the importance of comprehensive language processing capabilities. Additionally, technical glitches, such as bugs or errors in the AI software, can lead to unexpected behavior or crashes, further complicating interactions.

To effectively address these challenges, several troubleshooting techniques can be employed. First, clarifying queries is essential. Users should ensure their questions or commands are clear and specific, avoiding ambiguous language and providing context when necessary. This simple step can prevent many misunderstandings and improve the accuracy of AI responses.

Second, checking the system's status is a vital part of troubleshooting. Verifying that the AI system and its associated services are operational helps identify whether the issue lies with the user input or the system itself. Many platforms provide notifications or status updates that can inform users of ongoing maintenance or known issues.

Keeping software up to date is another critical practice. AI developers frequently release updates that include bug fixes, performance enhancements, and new features. Ensuring that the latest version of the AI software is installed can resolve many technical glitches and improve overall functionality.

Examining system logs is a more advanced troubleshooting step that provides insights into errors or warnings generated during operation. These logs can help pinpoint the source of a problem, enabling more targeted solutions. Consulting the system's documentation is equally valuable, as it often contains specific guidance on addressing common issues and optimizing performance.

Beyond troubleshooting, optimizing AI performance involves several strategies to enhance the system's efficiency and accuracy. Enhancing the training data is a foundational approach. Providing high-quality, diverse datasets helps the AI model learn effectively, enabling it to handle a broader range of scenarios and language variations. Developers should prioritize datasets that include real-world examples relevant to the intended use case.

Refining the underlying algorithms is another important optimization strategy. By reducing computational complexity and employing efficient data structures or parallel processing techniques, developers can significantly improve response times. Such refinements are particularly valuable for applications requiring real-time interaction.

Implementing caching mechanisms is an effective way to improve system efficiency. By storing frequently accessed data or responses, caching reduces the need for repeated computations, thereby decreasing response times and server load. This strategy is especially beneficial for high-traffic AI applications.

Continuous performance monitoring is also essential for identifying bottlenecks and areas for improvement. Metrics such as response time, accuracy, and resource usage provide actionable data that developers can use to fine-tune the system. Regular monitoring ensures that the AI remains effective as usage patterns and requirements evolve.

User feedback is a powerful tool for optimization. Encouraging users to share their experiences helps identify recurring issues and areas where the system can be improved. Integrating this feedback into the development process fosters a more user-centric AI system that aligns with real-world needs.

To illustrate these concepts, let's consider a few case studies. In one instance, a customer service chatbot struggled with accuracy, often providing irrelevant answers. By analyzing user queries and refining the training data, the development team improved the chatbot's accuracy by 30%. This improvement not only enhanced user satisfaction but also reduced the workload for human support agents.

In another case, an AI-powered recommendation system faced slow response times, frustrating users. The development team optimized the recommendation algorithm and implemented caching, reducing the average response time by 50%. This optimization significantly improved the user experience, increasing engagement with the platform.

A third case study involved a language translation AI that had difficulty handling slang and idiomatic expressions. By incorporating user feedback and expanding the training data to include more colloquial language, the system's translation accuracy improved markedly. This enhancement made the AI more accessible and reliable for diverse users.

Looking ahead, the field of AI troubleshooting and optimization is poised for further advancements. Automated debugging, where AI systems identify and resolve their own errors, is an emerging trend that promises to reduce the need for human intervention. Similarly, adaptive learning models that continuously evolve based on real-time interactions and feedback are becoming more prevalent, ensuring that AI systems remain relevant and effective in dynamic environments.

Edge computing is another promising development, enabling AI models to operate directly on edge devices rather than relying on centralized servers. This approach reduces latency and enhances performance, particularly for applications requiring real-time processing, such as autonomous vehicles or smart home devices.

By understanding and applying these troubleshooting and optimization strategies, users and developers can ensure more effective and efficient interactions with AI systems. These practices not only address current challenges but also pave the way for innovative applications and improved user experiences, cementing AI's role as a transformative technology.

Chapter 9: Future Trends in AI

As we stand on the brink of a new era in artificial intelligence, it's clear that the future holds exciting and transformative possibilities. This chapter explores some of the most promising trends and developments in AI that are expected to shape our world in the coming years. One of the most significant trends is the increasing collaboration between humans and AI. Rather than replacing human workers, AI is expected to augment human capabilities, leading to more efficient and innovative outcomes. This symbiotic relationship will be particularly evident in fields such as healthcare, education, and creative industries, where AI can assist with complex tasks, provide personalized recommendations, and even inspire new forms of artistic expression.

As AI systems become more integrated into our daily lives, the importance of ethical AI and responsible development cannot be overstated. Future trends will likely focus on creating transparent, fair, and accountable AI systems. This includes addressing biases in AI algorithms, ensuring data privacy, and developing frameworks for AI governance. The goal is to build trust in AI technologies and ensure they are used for the benefit of all. Additionally, ethical considerations in AI will likely drive the creation of global partnerships aimed at setting universal standards for AI use, ensuring inclusivity and fairness across diverse populations and industries.

Natural Language Processing (NLP) is another area poised for significant strides, enabling more natural and intuitive interactions between humans and machines. Future

AI systems will be able to understand and generate human language with greater accuracy and nuance, making communication with AI more seamless. This will enhance applications such as virtual assistants, customer service bots, and language translation tools. Beyond these, NLP advancements could enable AI to participate in complex debates, provide real-time sentiment analysis in diverse contexts, and foster cross-cultural communication by bridging language barriers effortlessly.

The healthcare sector is poised to benefit immensely from AI advancements. From early disease detection and personalized treatment plans to robotic surgeries and AI-driven drug discovery, the potential applications are vast. AI will help healthcare professionals make more informed decisions, improve patient outcomes, and streamline administrative processes. Future developments might include wearable AI devices capable of continuous health monitoring and systems that predict health crises before they occur, transforming preventative medicine into a more proactive and personalized discipline.

Similarly, the convergence of AI and the Internet of Things (IoT) will lead to smarter and more connected environments. AI-powered IoT devices will be able to collect and analyze data in real-time, enabling predictive maintenance, energy optimization, and enhanced security. Smart homes, cities, and industries will become more efficient and responsive to the needs of their inhabitants. For instance, AI could optimize traffic flow in smart cities, manage resource distribution more effectively, and enable entirely automated systems that reduce human intervention in routine operations.

Education is another area where AI is expected to make a significant impact. Personalized learning experiences, intelligent tutoring systems, and AI-driven educational content will cater to the unique needs of each student. This will help bridge learning gaps, foster a love for learning, and prepare students for the challenges of the future. Furthermore, AI can assist educators by analyzing learning patterns to provide insights into student performance, allowing for tailored approaches that maximize potential. Global access to quality education through AI-driven platforms could also become a reality, democratizing learning like never before.

AI also has the potential to play a crucial role in addressing environmental challenges. From optimizing energy usage and reducing waste to monitoring wildlife and predicting natural disasters, AI can help us create a more sustainable future. Innovative AI solutions will be essential in tackling climate change and preserving our planet for future generations. For example, AI could analyze vast datasets from satellites to detect deforestation, track illegal fishing, or identify pollution hotspots, offering actionable solutions to these pressing issues.

The advent of quantum computing promises to revolutionize AI by providing unprecedented computational power. Quantum computers will be able to solve complex problems that are currently beyond the reach of classical computers, leading to breakthroughs in fields such as cryptography, materials science, and artificial intelligence itself. The combination of quantum computing and AI will unlock new possibilities and accelerate technological progress. In the long term, quantum AI could enable discoveries in domains like genome sequencing and climate modeling, offering insights into challenges that currently remain unsolved.

Moreover, AI is set to become a valuable tool in the creative industries, assisting artists, musicians, writers, and designers in their work. AI algorithms can generate music, art, and literature, providing new sources of inspiration and collaboration. While AI-generated content will never replace human creativity, it will serve as a powerful complement, pushing the boundaries of what is possible. Collaborative projects between AI and human creators may yield entirely new art forms and challenge traditional notions of authorship.

In addition to creative fields, AI is likely to redefine the nature of work across multiple industries. Automation of repetitive tasks will free up human workers to focus on strategic and creative roles, fostering innovation and productivity. Future workplaces might also integrate AI-driven tools that enhance team collaboration, provide real-time feedback, and predict project outcomes, ensuring a more dynamic and efficient work environment.

AI's role in cybersecurity is another critical trend. With the growing complexity of cyber threats, AI-driven systems can detect, analyze, and mitigate risks faster than human analysts. Adaptive AI algorithms could also predict and neutralize potential threats before they materialize, ensuring the safety of sensitive data and critical infrastructures. These advancements will be instrumental in securing the rapidly expanding digital landscape.

Transportation is another sector poised for transformation through AI. Self-driving vehicles, powered by advanced AI, promise to revolutionize mobility, reducing accidents and increasing efficiency. AI could also optimize public transportation networks, ensuring more reliable and cost-effective services. In logistics, AI-powered systems will enhance supply chain management, from inventory control to delivery scheduling.

The integration of AI in entertainment will also see significant advancements. Personalized content recommendations, immersive virtual experiences, and AI-generated narratives will transform how we consume media. Additionally, AI-driven tools could enable real-time audience analysis, helping creators refine their content to better meet viewer preferences.

As AI continues to evolve, fostering public understanding and engagement will be vital. Educational campaigns and accessible resources can demystify AI, addressing misconceptions and promoting informed discussions about its capabilities and limitations. This inclusive approach will ensure that AI development aligns with societal values and priorities.

The future of AI is bright and full of potential. As we continue to explore and develop these technologies, it is essential to prioritize ethical considerations and ensure that AI serves the greater good. By embracing the opportunities and addressing the challenges, we can harness the power of AI to create a better, more connected, and sustainable world. This concludes our journey through the world of AI. As we look to the future, it is clear that AI will continue to evolve and shape our lives in profound ways. Stay curious, stay informed, and embrace the possibilities that lie ahead.